Poetry World
1

Poems collected by Geoffrey Summerfield
Illustrated by Per Dahlberg

Bell & Hyman

Published in 1985 by
Bell & Hyman Limited
Denmark House
37–39 Queen Elizabeth Street
London SE1 2QB

British Library Cataloguing in Publication Data

Poetry world.
 1
 1. English poetry
 I. Summerfield, Geoffrey
 821'.008'09282   PR1175

ISBN 0 7135 1517 1

Printed in Great Britain by
R. Hartnoll Limited, Bodmin, Cornwall

Contents

Oh, who will wash the tiger's ears?

Where do clowns go?

Sounds of the great sea

'Cool now' says the warm earth

By the full moonlight

The moon's in a fit

Poetry World I

It's dark in here

I am writing these poems
From inside a lion,
And it's rather dark in here.
So please excuse the handwriting
Which may not be too clear.
But this afternoon by the lion's cage
I'm afraid I got too near.
And I'm writing these lines
From inside a lion,
And it's rather dark in here.

Shel Silverstein

Bad Sir Brian Botany

Sir Brian had a battleaxe with great big knobs on;
He went among the villagers and blipped them on
        the head.
On Wednesday and on Saturday, but mostly on the
        latter day,
He called at all the cottages, and this is what he said:

    'I am Sir Brian!' (ting-ling)
    'I am Sir Brian!' (rat-tat)
    'I am Sir Brian, as bold as a lion—
    Take *that*!—and *that*!—and *that*!'

Sir Brian had a pair of boots with great big spurs on,
A fighting pair of which he was particularly fond.
On Tuesday and on Friday, just to make the street
        look tidy,
He'd collect the passing villagers and kick them in the
        pond.

    'I am Sir Brian!' (sper-lash!)
    'I am Sir Brian!' (sper-losh!)
    'I am Sir Brian, as bold as a lion—
    Is anyone else for a wash?'

Sir Brian woke one morning, and he couldn't find his
        battleaxe;
He walked into the village in his second pair of boots.
He had gone a hundred paces, when the street was full
        of faces,
And the villagers were round him with ironical salutes,

'You are Sir Brian? Indeed!
You are Sir Brian? Dear, dear!
You are Sir Brian, as bold as a lion?
Delighted to meet you here!'

Sir Brian went a journey, and he found a lot of duck-
       weed:
They pulled him out and dried him, and they blipped
       him on the head.
They took him by the breeches, and they hurled him
       into ditches,
And they pushed him under waterfalls, and this is what
       they said:

'You are Sir Brian—don't laugh,
You are Sir Brian—don't cry;
You are Sir Brian, as bold as a lion—
Sir Brian, the lion, good-bye!'

Sir Brian struggled home again, and chopped up his
       battleaxe,
Sir Brian took his fighting boots, and threw them in
       the fire.
He is quite a different person now he hasn't got his
       spurs on,
And he goes about the village as B. Botany, Esquire.

'I am Sir Brian? Oh, *no*!
I am Sir Brian? Who's he?
I haven't got any title, I'm Botany—
Plain Mr Botany (B).'

A. A. Milne

When good King Arthur ruled this land

When good King Arthur ruled this land,
He was a goodly king.
He stole three bags of barley-meal
To make a bag-pudding!

A big bag-pudding King Arthur made,
And stuffed it full of plums.
And in it he put great lumps of fat
As big as my two thumbs.

The King and Queen, they both tucked in
And all the court beside.
And what they couldn't eat that night,
The Queen next morning fried.

Traditional

Short stories

1
Punch and Judy
Fought for a pie.
Punch gave Judy
A smack in the eye.

2
There was an old woman,
Lived under a hill,
And if she's not gone,
She lives there still.

3
As Tommy Snooks and Bessy Brooks
Were walking out one Sunday
Said Tommy Snooks to Bessy Brooks:
'Tomorrow will be Monday.'

4
There was a boy went into a barn,
And lay down on the hay.
An owl came out and flew about.
And the boy ran, scared, away.

Traditional

Ickle Me, Pickle Me, Tickle Me too

Ickle Me, Pickle Me, Tickle Me too
Went for a ride in a flying shoe.
'Hooray!'
'What fun!'
'It's time we flew!'
Said Ickle Me, Pickle Me, Tickle Me too.

Ickle was captain, and Pickle was crew
And Tickle served coffee and mulligan stew
As higher
And higher
And higher they flew,
Ickle Me, Pickle Me, Tickle Me too.

Ickle Me, Pickle Me, Tickle Me too,
Over the sun and beyond the blue.
'Hold on!'
'Stay in!'
'I hope we do!'
Cried Ickle Me, Pickle Me, Tickle Me too.

Ickle Me, Pickle Me, Tickle Me too
Never returned to the world they knew,
And nobody
Knows what's
Happened to
Dear Ickle Me, Pickle Me, Tickle Me too.

Shel Silverstein

Noah's journey

I

The Building of The Ark

oak

is the keel. He is aged and
gnarl-faced. See, he is here
with his acorns and edged leaves.
Off with his bark and his big
roots. Oak is an old friend.
Lays down his light beams, dips
them in warm tar: submits to
a varnish on one side. Is all
washed and ready for when storm comes.

I am well-grained. I lie flat,
hold off the water and float on
the waves. Once grounded, I
wait for a sailing, alert in the sun.

pine

is the mast. He is upright,
smooth, straight and long-limbed.
He moves like a ramrod,
casting aside all his twigs and his
branches. A few cones
curling an eyebrow predict when the
rain's due. Standing in place now,
spun in a socket he sets like a
maypole. An oiled bole of red wood.

Screwed to the low deck, I
rise to the cold stars. The sea waits,
tossing a little. The black earth
lingers to wave me a long farewell.

II

Here are some of his passengers:

rat

> leaves a sinking ship. Wise
> brown rat, is there blame in that?
> If you have to leave the
> ark you must oar your way out
> with an ant and a ladybird
> aloft on your snout. Rat, make a
> ring, be a life-belt here.
> And gnaw me a port-hole or two
> to see through. That will keep you quiet.
>
> *Rough Noah, I will not. I prefer*
> *a biscuit. And as for sinking,*
> *why it doesn't bear thinking. I*
> *will nip your ankle if you nag at me.*

lynx

> is my look-out. He can see
> in the murk. Yellow falls the
> fog but the perk-eared lynx
> feels vigilant. On the branch of
> the mast he is pinned by his
> claws. Telescoped in muscle
> waits lynx for the land. With
> a leap he will land, be the
> first one on Ararat. Eh, peaked lynx?
>
> *I am anxious to rest my eyes.*
> *Keep me away from the dazzle of*
> *the zebra and the dots of the*
> *leopard. I will stare at the plain bear.*

pig

will need guiding with this
boar board. He is heavy with
acorns. Incontinent pig!
Why did they send me a pig
so big? You must learn to
be slimmer from the wolf or
the hare. I will fit you in
below decks. But you must keep
still, and not overlay any beast.

I am usefully fat. I can
keep some warm. There is sure
to be ice. And I shan't
need heat.

bear

are you there? Why, you smell
of honey. You voracious small bear!
Why have you come with your paws all
sticky? Go down to the sink.
You must dance for your
supper, and it won't be sweets.
Coarse brown bread for ominivorous
bears. And a beaker of brine
if we have to keep washing you in drinking water.

I am sorry, Noah. But I grew
quite faint. So I stopped by a hive
for a rest and a meal.
Let me give you a hug.

19

tiger

is a stick along railings. Like a
ripple in a lake he has lodged
in your eye. Come, tiger, you
are here. Tensed sinews in the rain.
Stretch out on the poop. Glare
over the orb of the ocean and
frighten the hail. We are safe,
mewed up in our tub with a
tiger to care for us. Tiger, look fierce.

With a roar and a bounce I
will tear up the clouds. Keep
plenty of meat, though, for me. I will
wait like a rug.

crocodile

creeps out of the swamp with a
creak and a snap. He is made like a
bag. He can float for a day
without winking his eye. In the mud
of the bayou he has pondered the flood
and decided to miss it. So come in,
long crocodile, and crawl to your space.
You can help make logs. We shall soon
need a fire. Lie there, and snap.

I would snap with a will. I have
toothache, though. Please, Noah, will you
give me a pill. In a mouth like mine
pain sprouts like a bush.

rhinoceros

comes aboard like a boulder. He is
lapped in hard layers like a
hot-water tank. We must study
him hard to improve the ark's
lagging. What a load you are
for us, lily-eared rhinoceros! If
you were to jump we should
plump to the bottom. Stand here
on this stout plank. And have some hay.

I don't eat hay. I am
sorry, I must say, to be such
a burden. Will it help if I lift
my little ox-pecker off?

elephant

comes last in his loose grey skin. In
the sun you can see brown
hairs on his back. I am sure he
will help to haul the ark
along the flat canal to the flood
when the water has come. He is
not forgetful of all the food
he will need. Have you brought green
leaves, ant-like and prudent elephant?

Aye, aye, Noah, I have hauled
this tree. It will feed huge me
for a year. Is there space
in the barge?

whale

must swim by the side of
the ship. If I take a dip
I can ride safe back on his
broad black head. Whale is
the biggest, are you not,
vast whale? In a storm you
can shelter the ship from the
waves. I will feed you for this
with plenty of plankton.

I am partial to plankton. I will
swim by your side. Yes, I will swim
by the ark's hind rim
and soothe the poor beasts who are sick.

III

The Battle with the Elements

thunder

> is the one who is blundering
> about. I can hear him in the
> sky like a lout in the attic.
> Bricks he would hurl if he
> had them. Bing. Bang. He is
> round like a gong with a
> big bronze face. Say boo to
> a goose he would not were it
> not for his flick-nosed cousin.

> *Talk big, small man, while you*
> *can. I will bash you. Just*
> *give me a minute to blow up*
> *my balloon. You wait.*

lightning

> is another. O another
> matter. Snears through the ether
> like a spear. Shrip-shrivels
> into shreds your elaborate
> ladders. Is a daze on the
> deck. Stiff blitz to the sheets.
> Fit scissors for the ropes
> of the bark's tossed body. In a fit
> you are cracked, split, ruined.

> *Nix, Noah, you exaggerate a*
> *little. You're afloat. I can*
> *see a green pug-dog awash in the stern*
> *but the fireworks are finished, I'm off.*

rain

is the one who goes on. He is flung
pita-pata-pita-pata from a
tipped bowl of dry peas. Wet fur,
wet wood, wet wings, wet canvas: the
whole wide world is awash in a
sluice of beans. Rattle, rush.
Down comes the roof in a slush
of cold glass bits. Below decks
glum beasts peer out and steam dry slowly.

I pour on. Always in
motion, a flow in the air, I
slither to all points. And fill earth
top-full of water, of water, of water.

wind

is the last one. A wild thing,
over the flat sea, the smooth
sea, he wanders. Whistling a
thin tune, a high tune, a shrill tune,
whirling the waves to a white, whizzed,
whipped-cream. Zing, zing, zing: and the
ark like a roundabout rolls up and
down, up and down, in a frenzy.
Packed close like sardines, the poor beasts are all sick.

I breathe on. Puffing my fat
cheeks, I fill the small ship's
sails: blow it towards sand,
send it to new shores.

George MacBeth

26

The broom-seller

A name for this I think I've got.
(I hope my mind don't fail!)
They call it—let me see—what? what?
Oh! Margery Tickletail!

Traditional

What in the world?

What in the world
　goes whiskery friskery
　　meowling and prowling
　　　napping and lapping
　　　　at silky milk?
Psst,
What is it?

What in the world
　goes leaping and beeping
　　onto a lily pad onto a log
　　　onto a tree stump or down to the bog?
Splash, blurp,
Kerchurp!

What in the world
　goes gnawing and pawing
　　scratching and latching
　　　sniffing and squiffing
　　　　nibbling for tidbits of left-over cheese?
Please?

What in the world
　jumps with a hop and a bump
　　and a tail that can thump
　　　has pink pointy ears and a twitchy nose
　　　　looking for anything crunchy that grows?
A carroty lettucey cabbagey luncheon
To munch on?

What in the world
   climbs chattering pattering swinging from trees
      like a flying trapeze
         with a tail that can curl
            like the rope cowboys twirl?
Wahoo!
Here's a banana for you!

What in the world
   goes stalking and balking
      running and sunning
         thumping and dumping
            lugging and hugging
               swinging and singing
                  wriggling and giggling
                     sliding and hiding
                        throwing and knowing and
                        growing and growing
                           much too big for
                              last year's clothes?
Who knows?

Eve Merriam

Scots riddles

1

My head is up on a height:
Hills lie between my feet:
My father is all light:
My mother is all wet.

2

Longlegged Lanky crosses the floor,
With his only leg in the air.
Outside the door he shakes his head,
The dust from his hair to shed.

3

I'm a thing. I'm nothing.
Both a big and small thing:
I belong to everything.

4

Lizzy with her curly frills,
So slender and so spry,
When the night creeps over the hills,
She always starts to cry.

Always cries so bitterly
After we've had our dinner,
Though all her hair hangs prettily,
And she has a clean white pinna!

5
Although it runs
It cannot walk:
Although it turns
It can't go back.
Although it falls
It cannot break:
Although it calls
It cannot speak.

6
Oh, he's really absurd!
He stands on his head.
Says never a word
Though for words he was made.

He slides on his nose;
Back and forth he goes;
What he says is never heard.
Yet the deaf catch every word.

7
I'm sure you know the great big house
Whose walls are ever so high,
Where in the shadows many a mouse
Peeps out with twinkling eye.

And I'm sure you know the great big cat
Who cannily tiptoes in:
Sometimes she's incredibly fat,
And sometimes amazingly thin!

Answers: *1 Rainbow. 2 Broom. 3 Shadow. 4 Candle.*
5 Stream. 6 Pen or pencil. 7 Night sky, with stars and moon.

William Soutar

A fishy square dance

Tuna turn,
flounder round,
cuttlefish up,
halibut hold;

clam and salmon
trout about,
terrapin,
shrimp dip in;

forward swordfish,
mackerel back,
dace to the left,
ide to the right;

gallop scallop,
mussel perch,
grunnion run,
bass on down;

finnan haddie,
skate and fluke,
eel and sole,
shad and roe;

haddock, herring,
hake, squid, pike:
cod promenade
and lobster roll!

Eve Merriam

Little fish

The tiny fish enjoy themselves
in the sea.
Quick little splinters of life,
their little lives are fun to them
in the sea.

D. H. Lawrence

The hare

In the black furrow of a field
I saw an old witch-hare this night;
And she cocked a lissome ear,
And she eyed the moon so bright,
And she nibbled of the green;
And I whispered 'Whsst! Witch-hare!'
Away like a ghostie o'er the field
She fled, and left the moonlight there.

Walter de la Mare

Fieldmouse

Fieldmouse scampers,
Heart a-burning,
Machine rumbles,
Blades a-whirring,
Terror pushing,
Blindly faster
Thoughtless-heedless,
Stops—heart-a-busting
Machine rumbles,
Blades a-whirring
Bloody harvest.

Nigel Cullum

A pig tale

Poor Jane Higgins,
She had five piggins,
And one got drowned in the Irish Sea.
Poor Jane Higgins,
She had four piggins,
And one flew over a sycamore tree.
Poor Jane Higgins,
She had three piggins,
And one was taken away for pork.
Poor Jane Higgins,
She had two piggins,
And one was sent to the Bishop of Cork.
Poor Jane Higgins,
She had one piggin,
And that was struck by a shower of hail,
So poor Jane Higgins,
She had no piggins,
And that's the end of my little pig tale.

James Reeves

Black-out

The flippered mole
With his frilled snout
Furrows and burrows
His way about.

With feet like fins
He swims in loam
And with his whiskers
Lights his home.

Dilys Laing

Who really?

When Winter's o'er, the Bear once more
Rolls from his hollow tree
And pokes about, and in and out,
Where dwells the honey-bee.
Then all the little creatures go,
And to their Queen they say:
'Here's that old Bruin, hark, what he's doing,
Let's drive the beast away!'
Old Bruin smiles, and smoothes his hair
Over his sticky nose;
'That Thieves should hate a Thief,' he smirks,
'Who really would suppose!'

Walter de la Mare

Stop, thief!

The false fox came to our house one night
And gave all the geese a terrible fright.

He came on tiptoe through the gate.
The geese were in a dreadful state.

He took a fat goose fast by the neck.
The poor goose cried out 'Queck! Queck! Queck!'

My mother ran out all alone
And at the fox she threw a stone.

My father ran out with a pail
And hit the fox—Clank!—on his tail.

But false fox had his goosey-gander
And away he ran with his precious plunder.

He carried the goose off to his lair,
And all his family had a share.

Then, lo and behold, he came back next week—
Who'd have thought he'd have the cheek!

He came sneaking as quiet as a mouse
And stole two chickens from behind the house!

When he got home he said to his wife
'A fox's life is a merry life!'

Anon. Rewritten by Geoffrey Summerfield

To a squirrel at Kyle-na-no

Come play with me;
Why should you run
Through the shaking tree
As though I'd a gun
To strike you dead?
When all I would do
Is to scratch your head
And let you go.

W. B. Yeats

The Yak

There was a most odious Yak
Who took only toads on his Back:
If you asked for a Ride,
He would act very Snide,
And go humping off, yicketty-yak.

Theodore Roethke

What became of them?

He was a rat, and she was a rat,
    And down in one hole they did dwell,
And both were as black as a witch's cat,
    And they loved one another well.

He had a tail, and she had a tail,
    Both long and curling and fine;
And each said, 'Yours is the finest tail
    In the world, excepting mine.'

He smelt the cheese, and she smelt the cheese,
    And they both pronounced it good;
And both remarked it would greatly add
    To the charms of their daily food.

So he ventured out, and she ventured out,
    And I saw them go with pain;
For what befell them I never can tell,
    For they never came back again.

Anon.

I saw a jolly hunter

I saw a jolly hunter
  With a jolly gun
Walking in the country
  In the jolly sun.

In the jolly meadow
  Sat a jolly hare.
Saw the jolly hunter.
  Took jolly care.

Hunter jolly eager—
  Sight of jolly prey.
Forgot gun pointing
  Wrong jolly way.

Jolly hunter jolly head
  Over heels gone.
Jolly old safety catch
  Not jolly on.

Bang went the jolly gun.
  Hunter jolly dead.
Jolly hare got clean away.
  Jolly good, I said.

Charles Causley

Hi!

Hi! handsome hunting man
Fire your little gun.
Bang! Now the animal
Is dead and dumb and done.
Nevermore to peep again, creep again, leap again,
Eat or sleep or drink again, Oh, what fun!

Walter de la Mare

My pet frog

I have a great big, slimey frog.
I found him underneath a log.
Though greasy, oily, fat as lard,
When he stirs he leaps a yard.

He's yellow-green with spots of brown,
A heaving, glistening, mottled gown.
He puffs and blows—he must be old.
Whatever the weather he's always cold.

But when he sits on the edge of the pool
As to show that he's no fool,
In he dives with scarcely a plop.
What a display (without swallowing a drop!).

Simon Blackburn, 8

Oliphaunt

Grey as a mouse,
Big as a house,
Nose like a snake,
I make the earth shake,
As I tramp through the grass;
Trees crack as I pass.
With horns in my mouth
I walk in the South,
Flapping big ears.
Beyond count of years
I stump round and round,
Never lie on the ground,
Not even to die.
Oliphaunt am I,
Biggest of all,
Huge, old, and tall.
If ever you'd meet me,
You wouldn't forget me.
If you never do,
You won't think I'm true;
But old Oliphaunt am I,
And I never lie.

J. R. R. Tolkien

Alas, alack!

Ann, Ann!
   Come! quick as you can!
There's a fish that *talks*
   In the frying-pan.
Out of the fat,
   As clear as glass,
He put up his mouth
   And moaned 'Alas!'
Oh, most mournful,
   'Alas, alack!'
Then turning to his sizzling,
   And sank him back.

Walter de la Mare

God bless

A little boy kneels at the foot of the bed
Saying his evening prayers.
'Dear God, please will you tell my mummy
I'm sorry I pushed her downstairs.
And if my auntie's up there with you
Will you please tell her I'm sorry too,
I didn't know that she would die
If I put poison in the pie,
About the man in the bowler hat,
I didn't mean to shoot his cat.
Sister Jane has gone away
All because she wouldn't play,
I weighed her down with great big rocks
And put her in a wooden box
And then I pushed it in the sea.
I don't think she came home to tea.
And God, I'm really awfully sorry
I pushed poor Charlie under a lorry.
So God bless anyone alive,
It's time, I think, I learnt to drive.'

Peter Tinsley, 13

Quick! Quick!

Quick, quick, the cat's been sick!
Where, where?
Under the chair!
Hasten, hasten, fetch a basin!
Oh, Kate, Kate! You're far too late!
The carpet's in a dreadful state!

Traditional

The acrobats

I'll swing
By my ankles,
She'll cling
To your knees
As you hang
By your nose
From a high-up
Trapeze.
But just one thing, please,
As we float through the breeze—
Don't sneeze.

Shel Silverstein

Old Dame Trot and her cat

Old Dame Trot
Went to the fair,
With her cat on her shoulder,
To see the people there.

Dame Trot and her cat
Sat down for a chat.
The Dame sat on this side,
The cat sat on that.
'Can you catch a rat
Or a mouse in the dark?'
'Purr' said the cat.

Dame Trot went for apples
And sugar and spice.
When she came back
Puss was playing with mice.

She went out to buy her
A smart new hat.
When she came back
Puss was hunting a rat.

She trotted once more
To buy a jam tart.
When she came back
Puss was dressed very smart.

'You look nice now you're dressed,'
Says old Dame Trot
Puss curtseyed and mewed,
And that was the lot.

Traditional

The celebrated cat, Purser O'Hara

From a Cats' Home we one day got
A long-haired Kit with many a spot;
A good one too; but O what fleas,
And how his snuffling snoot did wheeze,
And O how long we had to toil
With brush and comb and castor-oil,
And capsules for the hated worm,
To get the blighter into form!
And O how long his manners took,
So that he must be brought to book
With slaps and scolding twice a day
Before he'd tread the narrow way!
You see, the thing could hardly lap;
He missed his mother, poor old chap.
But he was strong, he found his feet,
Began to think his food a treat;
And (how it happened no one knew)
He simply grew and grew and grew.
Perhaps it was the ample food;
We like to think 'twas gratitude.

At three months, big as full-grown cat,
Which all the neighbours wondered at;
At six months, fourteen pounds he weighed,
Which all the other cats dismayed;
Yet undiscouraged he went on
Till pounds he numbered twenty-one
At three years old: in two years more
He made his top score, twenty-four.

It's nice to have a cat that's fat.
At least, a cat as fat as that.
He had such spreading, fusby feet;
He had a bottom you could beat;
He loved a rough-house, and would spring
And rush about like anything.
You see, he need not be afraid,
Like small cats delicately made.
And when downstairs he'd run and jump
His feet like football-boots would thump.
We used to carry him about,
Draped round our necks, and take him out,
And those beholding him said "Cor!"
As though expecting him to roar.

He died before the beastly Blitz,
Which would have scared him into fits,
And (bar the start) his life was passed
In Fun and Games from first to last.

Ruth Pitter

Cat's song

Up there on the roof tops
Sit the cats yowling
Screaming and howling
And singing such wonderful songs
Topsy and Timmy are singing with Jimmy
Tingy and Leppy are singing together
Goldy and Silver chorus with Dover
While Domino sings by herself.

Wendy Hancock

Cat's appetite

You can keep a cat, and feed him well with milk
And the best of meat, and make him a bed of silk,
But just let him see a mouse run along the wall
And he'll leave the milk and meat and all—
Every luxury, no matter how nice,—
So passionate is his love of mice!

Anon. Rewritten by Geoffrey Summerfield

The sage

The cat is eating the roses:
that's the way he is.
Don't stop him, don't stop
the world going round,
that's the way things are.
The third of May
was misty; fourth of May
who knows. Sweep
the rose-meat up, throw the bits
out in the rain.
He never eats
every crumb, says
the hearts are bitter.
That's the way he is, he knows
the world and the weather.

Denise Levertov

My cats
(a witch speaks)

I like to toss him up and down
A heavy cat weighs half a crown
With a hey ho diddle my cat Brown.

I like to pinch him on the sly
When nobody is passing by
With a hey ho diddle my cat Fry.

I like to ruffle up his pride
And watch him skip and turn aside
With a hey ho diddle my cat Hyde.

Hey Brown and Fry and Hyde my cats
That sit on tombstones for your mats.

Stevie Smith

Roger the dog

Asleep he wheezes at his ease.
He only wakes to scratch his fleas.

He hogs the fire, he bakes his head
As if it were a loaf of bread.

He's just a sack of snoring dog.
You can lug him like a log.

You can roll him with your foot,
He'll stay snoring where he's put.

I take him out for exercise,
He rolls in cowclap up to his eyes.

He will not race, he will not romp,
He saves his strength for gobble and chomp.

He'll work as hard as you could wish
Emptying his dinner dish,

Then flops flat, and digs down deep,
Like a miner, into sleep.

Ted Hughes

Down behind the dustbin

Down behind the dustbin
I met a dog called Ted.
'Leave me alone,' he says,
'I'm just going to bed.'

Down behind the dustbin
I met a dog called Felicity.
'It's a bit dark here,' she said,
'They've cut off the electricity.'

Down behind the dustbin
I met a dog called Roger.
'Do you own this bin?' I said.
'No. I'm only the lodger.'

Ian said,
Down behind the dustbin
I met a dog called Sue.
'What are you doing here?' I said.
'I've got nothing else to do.'

Down behind the dustbin
I met a dog called Anne.
'I'm just off now,' she said,
'to see a dog about a man.'

Down behind the dustbin
I met a dog called Jack.
'Are you going anywhere?' I said.
'No. I'm just coming back.'

Down behind the dustbin
I met a dog called Billy.
'I'm not talking to you,' I said,
'if you're going to be silly.'

Down behind the dustbin
I met a dog called Barry.
He tried to take the bin away
but it was too heavy to carry.

Down behind the dustbin
I met a dog called Mary.
'I wish I wasn't a dog,' she said,
'I wish I was a canary.'

Michael Rosen

The song of the dustbin

Wrap it up in papery wapery
All the junk and dapery lapery,
Get rid of all the wasty gapery
Dirty, donty, dooth.
Clankily clonkily goes the donkery
Inkery bankery went the ronkily,
Taking out of all the rubbishly
Slimey, slonky, slooth.
Thinkery thonkery thought the thunkily
Slithy slothy went the lunkily,
Crashing all the zinkily zunkily
Mingle, mangle, mooth.

Here's the dustman thompy thumpery
Come to get the bins for umpery,
Carry them on their backsy bumpery
Jogery, jamily, jooth.
Put it in the lorryly loomily
Start it up quonkily quoomily,
Down the road screechy scroomily
Finkily, fonkily, footh.
Turn the corner sharpily soothily
Now we're at the dumpy doothily,
Empty it on the rest of the mungily
Kunkily, konkery, kooth.
There it lies for many a century
Going all bad and rotting rentury,
Twenty yards and pooey pongery
Camily, comily, cooth.

Here's a bulldozer faloomfily flomithily
Come to now the dumpy doothily,
Never again to nothily noothily
This is the song of the dustbin.

Michael Scott, 14

Eletelephony

Once there was an elephant
Who tried to use the telephant—
No! No! I mean an elephone
Who tried to use the telephone—
(Dear me! I am not certain quite
That even now I've got it right).

Howe'er it was, he got his trunk
Entangled in the telephunk;
The more I tried to get it free,
The louder buzzed the telephee—
(I fear I'd better drop the song
Of elephop and telephong!)

Laura Richards

It was a stormy night

It was a stormy night
One Christmas day
as they fell awake
on the Santa Fe

Turkey, jelly
and the ship's old cook
all jumped out
of a recipe book

The jelly wobbled
the turkey gobbled
and after them both
the old cook hobbled

Gobbler gobbled
Hobbler's Wobbler.
Hobbler gobbled
Wobbler's Gobbler.

Gobbly-gobbler
gobbled Wobbly
Hobbly-hobbler
Gobbled Gobbly.

Gobble gobbled
Hobble's Wobble
Hobble gobbled
gobbled Wobble.

gobble gobble
wobble wobble
hobble gobble
wobble gobble

Michael Rosen

Did you ever, ever, ever

Did you ever, ever, ever,
In your leaf, loaf, life
See the deavil, doavil, devil
Kiss his weaf, woaf, wife?

No, I never, never, never
In my leaf, loaf, life
Saw the deavil, doavil, devil
Kiss his weaf, woaf, wife!

Traditional

Cuckoo

In April,
Come he will.

In May,
He sings all day.

In June,
Changes his tune.

In July,
Makes ready to fly.

In August,
Go he must.

Traditional

The Bubblyjock, or Turkeycock

Half bogey and half bird,
He hiccups long and loud.
He stretches his jaws so wide
It's a wonder he doesn't explode!

He can't get that tune to roll,
Though he twists his neck like a snake,
'Cause he's swallowed the bagpipes whole
And the bag's stuck fast in his clack!

Translated from the Scots of Hugh MacDiarmid by Geoffrey
Summerfield

On the grass

Goose running along the lane:
Shadow, too, running along the lane.

Goose running over the lawn:
Shadow, too, running over the lawn.

White goose and her shadow,
Running . . . running . . . running.

And . . . into the water she goes!

Miyoshi Tatsuji

Jenny Wren

As little Jenny Wren
Was sitting on the shed,
She waggled her tail
And nodded her head.

And then she fell sick
But wasting no time
Robin Redbreast came quick
And brought her some wine.

'Get well soon, dear Jenny,
And drink up your wine.'
'Thanks, Robin, kindly!
Now you shall be mine.'

Then Jenny got well.
She stood on her feet,
And told Robin straight
She loved him not a bit.

Robin was angry
And hopped on a branch,
Shouting, 'Oh how could you!
Shame on you, unkind wench!'

Traditional

The death of Jenny Wren

Jenny Wren fell ill again,
And Jenny Wren did die,
Though doctors said they'd cure her
Or know the reason why.

Doctor Hawk felt her pulse
And shaking his head
Said 'I'm afraid I can't save her
Because she's quite dead.'

Doctor Owl then declared
That the cause of her death
He really believed was—
She ran out of breath!

Traditional

Crumbs

You little birds, I bring my crumbs,
For now the cold of winter comes.
The North Wind blows down frozen rain;
The fields are white with snow again;
The worm's in house; the bare-twigged trees
Are thick with frost instead of bees;
From running brooks all noise is gone;
And every pool lies still as stone.

Walter de la Mare

Oh, who will wash the tiger's ears?

Oh, who will wash the tiger's ears?
And who will comb his tail?
And who will brush his sharp white teeth?
And who will file his nails?

Oh, Bobby may wash the tiger's ears
And Susy may file his nails
And Lucy may brush his long white teeth
And I'll go down for the mail.

Shel Silverstein

At the playground

Away down deep and away up high,
A swing drops you into the sky.
Back, it draws you away down deep,
forth, it flings you in a sweep
all the way to the stars and back
—Goodby, Jill; Goodby, Jack:
Shuddering climb wild and steep,
away up high, away down deep.

William Stafford

Allie

Allie, call the birds in,
   The birds from the sky!
Allie calls, Allie sings,
   Down they all fly:
First there came
Two white doves,
   Then a sparrow from his nest,
Then a clucking bantam hen,
   Then a robin red-breast.

Allie, call the beasts in,
   The beasts, every one!
Allie calls, Allie sings,
   In they all run:
First there came
Two black lambs,
   Then a grunting Berkshire sow,
Then a dog without a tail,
   Then a red and white cow.

Allie, call the fish up,
   The fish from the stream!
Allie calls, Allie sings,
   Up they all swim:
First there came
Two gold fish,
   A minnow and a miller's thumb,
Then a school of little trout,
   Then the twisting eels come.

Allie, call the children,
    Call them from the green!
Allie calls, Allie sings,
    Soon they run in:
First there came
Tom and Madge,
    Kate and I who'll not forget
How we played by the water's edge
    Till the April sun set.

Robert Graves

See saw

Days are bright,
Nights are dark.
We play see saw
In the park.

Look at me.
And my friend
Freckle Face
The other end.

Shiny board
Between my legs.
Feet crunch down
On the twigs.

I crouch close
To the ground
Till it's time,
And up I bound.

Legs go loose,
Legs go tight.
I drop down
Like the night.

Like a scales,
Give and take,
Take and give.
My legs ache.

So it ends
As it begins.
Off we climb
And no one wins!

Thom Gunn

Solitude

I have a house where I go
When there's too many people,
I have a house where I go
Where no one can be;
I have a house where I go,
Where nobody ever says 'No';
Where no one says anything—so
     There is no one but me.

A. A. Milne

The departure

Have you got the moon safe?
Please, tie those strings a little tighter.
This loaf, push it down further
the light is crushing it—such a baguette
golden brown and so white inside
you don't see every day
nowadays. And for God's sake
don't let's leave in the end
without the ocean! Put it
in there among the shoes, and
tie the moon on behind. It's time!

Denise Levertov

Magic

Sandra's seen a leprechaun,
Eddie touched a troll,
Laurie danced with witches once,
Charlie found some goblin's gold.
Donald heard a mermaid sing,
Susy spied an elf,
But all the magic I have known
I've had to make myself.

Shel Silverstein

Invisible boy

And here we see the invisible boy
In his lovely invisible house,
Feeding a piece of invisible cheese
To a little invisible mouse.
Oh, what a beautiful picture to see!
Will you draw an invisible picture for me?

Shel Silverstein

Henry and Mary

Henry was a young king,
   Mary was his queen;
He gave her a snowdrop
   On a stalk of green.

Then all for his kindness
   And for all his care
She gave him a new-laid egg
   In the garden there.

'Love, can you sing?'
             'I cannot sing.'
  'Or tell a tale?'
           'Not one I know.'
'Then let us play at queen and king
   As down the garden walks we go.'

Robert Graves

Boa constrictor

Oh, I'm being eaten
By a boa constrictor,
A boa constrictor,
A boa constrictor,
I'm being eaten by a boa constrictor,
And I don't like it—one bit.
Well, what do you know?
It's nibblin' my toe.
Oh, gee,
It's up to my knee.
Oh my,
It's up to my thigh.
Oh, fiddle,
It's up to my middle.
Oh, heck,
It's up to my neck.
Oh, dread,
It's upmmmmmmmmmmmfffffffffff. . .

Shel Silverstein

If I had forty horsemen

If I had forty horsemen
I'd dress them in a row
And send them off by bugle call
To farthest Jericho.

And stand and watch them pass me,
Their scarlet plumes outthrust,
Their silver shoes a-flashing,
A-flashing in the dust.

And when the dust had settled
And I was all alone,
I'd telegraph, 'Immediate:
Top Secret: Now come home!'

James Britton

A fishing song

There was a boy whose name was Phinn,
And he was fond of fishing;
His father could not keep him in,
Nor all his mother's wishing.

His life's ambition was to land
A fish of several pounds weight.
The chief thing he could understand
Was hooks, or worms for bait.

The worms crept out, the worms crept in,
From every crack and pocket.
He had a worm-box made of tin,
With proper worms to stock it.

He gave his mind to breeding worms
As much as he was able.
His sister spoke in angry terms
To see them on the table.

You found one walking up the stairs,
You found one in a bonnet,
Or, in the bed-room, unawares,
You set your foot upon it.

With rod and line to Twickenham Ait
Tomorrow he is trudging.
Worms, worms, worms for bait!
Roach, and dace, and gudgeon!

W. B. Rands

Cottage

When I live in a Cottage
I shall keep in my Cottage

Two different Dogs,
Three creamy Cows,
Four giddy Goats,
Five Pewter Pots
Six silver Spoons
Seven busy Beehives
Eight ancient Appletrees
Nine red Rosebushes
Ten teeming Teapots
Eleven chirping Chickens
Twelve cosy Cats with their kittenish Kittens and
One blessèd Baby in a Basket.

That's what I'll have when I live in my Cottage.

Eleanor Farjeon

Cider in the potting-shed

I'm sitting in the Potting-shed
   Listening to the rain.
The tiles are streaming overhead,
   The garden breathes again:
The summer cabbages outside
   Are drumming to the drops,
So here will you and I abide
   And drink until it stops.

I'll sit upon this heap of mould,
   You on that pile of sand,
And each of us shall firmly hold
   A tankard in his hand.
And so that neither one shall be
   Disturbed or put about,
The boy who brought the cider, he
   Shall stand and pour it out.

And here's your bit of bread and cheese,
   And here likewise is mine.
Look at the bloomy Apple-trees,
   They twinkle and they shine;
The rainbow is above the wood
   Beyond the garden wall,
And near and far, in solitude,
   The Maytime cuckoos call.

Ruth Pitter

Don't try to be funny

I tried to make him laugh
By standing on my head

I tried to make him laugh
By rushing what I said

I tried to make him laugh
By sawing up the bed

I tried to make him laugh
By grunting while I read

I tried to make him laugh
By saying I was dead

I tried to make him laugh
By pulling down the shed

I tried to make him laugh—
But I laughed at him instead.

A. Patterson, 13

Jack the Piper

As I was going up the hill
I met with Jack the Piper,
And all the tunes that he could play
Was 'Tie up your petticoats tighter.'

I tied them once, I tied them twice,
I tied them three times over,
And all the songs that he could sing
Was 'Carry me safe to Dover.'

Traditional

There was a man and he had nought

There was a man, and he had nought,
And robbers came to rob him.
He crept up to the chimney pot
And then they thought they had him.

But he got down the other side,
And then they could not find him.
He ran fourteen miles in fifteen days,
And never looked behind him.

Traditional

My dad's thumb

My dad's thumb
can stick pins in wood
without flinching —
it can crush family-size matchboxes
in one stroke
and lever off jam-jar lids without piercing
at the pierce here sign.

If it wanted
it could be a bath-plug
or a paint-scraper
a keyhole cover or a tap-tightener.

It's already a great nutcracker
and if it dressed up
it could easily pass
as a broad bean or a big toe.

In actual fact, it's quite simply
the world's fastest envelope burster.

Michael Rosen

My Aunt Jane

My Aunt Jane she took me in.
She gives me tea out of her wee tin,
Half a bap, and a wee snow-top,
Three black lumps out of her wee shop.

My Aunt Jane she's awful smart,
She bakes me rings in an apple-tart,
And when Hallowe'en comes round
Presents that tart, I'm always bound.

My Aunt Jane has a bell on the door
And a white stone-step, and a clean-swept floor,
Candy apples, hard green pears,
Conversation lozenges!

My Aunt Jane she took me in.
She gives me tea out of her wee tin,
Half a bap, and a wee snow-top,
Three black lumps out of her wee shop.

Traditional

Baby Bella

Baby Bella, can she hear
All the saucy names I call her,
Puss, and Puck, and Darling dear,
Monkey, Mouse, and Squally-bawler!
Idle fly, Pigeon-pie—
(How I wish that I could hold her,)
Sugar-sucker! Bib-and-tucker!
Laughing at me as I scold her!

Gerda Fay

Clowns

Where do clowns go,
what do clowns eat,
where do clowns sleep,

what do clowns do,
when nobody,
just nobody laughs
any more,
Mummy?

Miroslav Holub

Gipsy Jane

She had corn-flowers in her ear,
As she came up the lane.
'What may be your name, my dear?'—
'O, sir, Gipsy Jane.'

'You are berry-brown, my dear'—
'That, sir, well may be.
For I live, more than half the year,
Under tent or tree.'

Shine, Sun! Blow, Wind!
Fall gently, Rain!
The year's declined. Be soft and kind,
Kind to Gipsy Jane.

W. B. Rands

An old woman sat spinning

An old woman sat spinning
And that's the beginning.
She had a calf
And that's half.
And she went to a ball,
And that's all.

Traditional

Hungry waters

The old men of the sea
With their seaweedy hair
Have scratched at the coast
Like a greedy bear.

They gobble up the castles,
Chew mountains to sand
And soon they'll have swallowed
The whole of the land.

Licking their white lips,
And roaring like a bear,
The old men of the sea
With their seaweed hair.

Translated from the Scots of Hugh MacDiarmid by Geoffrey
Summerfield

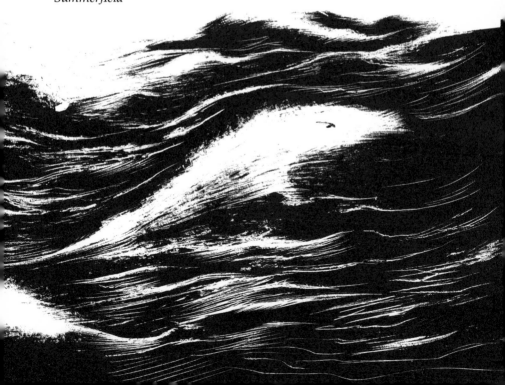

Grim and gloomy

Oh, grim and gloomy,
So grim and gloomy
Are the caves beneath the sea.
Oh, rare but roomy
And bare and boomy,
Those salt sea caverns be.

Oh, slim and slimy
Or grey and grimy
Are the animals of the sea.
Salt and oozy
And safe and snoozy
The caves where those animals be.

Hark to the shuffling,
Huge and snuffling,
Ravenous, cavernous, great sea-beasts!
But fair and fabulous,
Tintinnabulous,
Gay and fabulous are their feasts.

Ah, but the queen of the sea,
The querulous, perilous sea!
How the curls of her tresses
The pearls on her dresses,
Sway and swirl in the waves,
How cosy and dozy,
How sweet ring a-rosy
Her bower in the deep-sea caves!

Oh, rare but roomy
And bare and boomy
Those caverns under the sea,
And grave and grandiose,
Safe and sandiose
The dens of her denizens be.

James Reeves

Minnie and Winnie

Minnie and Winnie
  Slept in a shell.
Sleep, little ladies!
  And they slept well.

Pink was the shell within,
  Silver without;
Sounds of the great sea
  Wandered about.

Sleep, little ladies!
  Wake not soon!
Echo on echo
  Dies to the moon. . . .

Alfred, Lord Tennyson

Advice to young children

'Children who paddle where the ocean bed shelves steeply
Must take care they do not
Paddle too deeply.'

Thus spake the awful aging couple
Whose heart the years had turned to rubble.

But the little children, to save any bother,
Let it in one ear and out at the other.

Stevie Smith

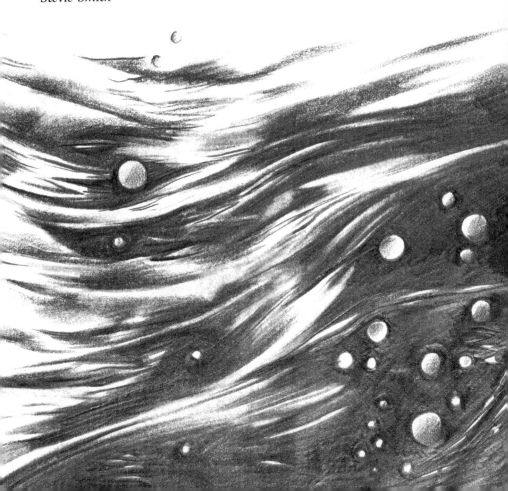

Spanish gold

When I was young I used to hold
   I'd run away to sea,
And be a Pirate brave and bold
   On the coast of Caribbee.

For I sez to meself, 'I'll fill me hold
With Spanish silver and Spanish gold,
And out of every ship I sink
I'll collar the best of food and drink.

'For Caribbee, or Barbaree,
Or the shores of South Amerikee
Are all the same to a Pirate bold,
Whose thoughts are fixed on Spanish gold.'

So one fine day I runs away
   A Pirate for to be;
But I found there was never a Pirate left
   On the coast of Caribbee.

For Pirates go, but their next of kin
Are Merchant Captains, hard as sin,
And Merchant Mates as hard as nails
Aboard of every ship that sails.

And I worked aloft and I worked below,
I worked wherever I had to go,
And the winds blew hard and the winds blew cold.
And I sez to meself as the ship she rolled,

'O Caribbee! O Barbaree!
O shores of South Amerikee!
O, never go there: if the truth be told,
You'll get more kicks than Spanish gold.'

Norman Lindsay

The months

January brings the snow,
Makes our feet and fingers glow.

February brings the rain,
Thaws the frozen lake again.

March brings breezes loud and shrill,
Stirs the dancing daffodil.

April brings the primrose sweet,
Scatters daisies at our feet.

May brings flocks of pretty lambs,
Skipping by their fleecy dams.

June brings tulips, lilies, roses,
Fills the children's hands with posies.

Hot July brings cooling showers,
Apricots and gillyflowers.

August brings the sheaves of corn,
Then the harvest home is borne.

Warm September brings the fruit,
Sportsmen then begin to shoot.

Fresh October brings the pheasant,
Then to gather nuts is pleasant.

Dull November brings the blast,
Then the leaves are whirling fast.

Chill December brings the sleet,
Blazing fire and Christmas treat.

Sara Coleridge

June

'Cool now' says the warm earth, and sighs.
'Quiet now' say the trees with barely a murmur
Rustling their leaves.
Small now, under a single sheet,
I am a child lying in bed.
Quiet.
Cool.

James Britton

John Mouldy

I spied John Mouldy in his cellar,
Deep down twenty steps of stone;
In the dusk he sat a-smiling,
   Smiling there alone.

He read no book, he snuffed no candle;
The rats ran in, the rats ran out;
And far and near, the drip of water
   Went whispering about.

The dusk was still, with dew a-falling,
I saw the Dog-star bleak and grim,
I saw a slim brown rat of Norway
   Creep over him.

I spied John Mouldy in his cellar,
Deep down twenty steps of stone;
In the dusk he sat a-smiling,
   Smiling there alone.

Walter de la Mare

Fair Rosa

Fair Rosa was a lovely child, a lovely child, a lovely child,
A long time ago.

A wicked fairy cast a spell, cast a spell, cast a spell,
A long time ago.

Fair Rosa slept for a hundred years, a hundred years,
            a hundred years,
A long time ago.

The hedges they all grew around, grew around, grew
            around,
A long time ago.

A handsome prince came a-riding by, a-riding by,
            a-riding by,
A long time ago.

He cut the hedges one by one, one by one, one by one,
A long time ago.

He kissed Fair Rosa's lily-white hand, lily-white hand,
            lily-white hand,
A long time ago.

Fair Rosa will not sleep no more, sleep no more, sleep
            no more,
A long time ago.

Traditional

The little bright one

Where the little
bright one runs
sparks fly.
He has the sun's
fire in his feet
and where he sprints
all the stones
are flints.

Dilys Laing

The ride-by-nights

Up on their brooms the Witches stream,
Crooked and black in the crescent's gleam;
One foot high, and one foot low,
Bearded, cloaked, and cowled, they go.
'Neath Charlie's Wane they twitter and tweet,
And away they swarm 'neath the Dragon's feet.
With a whoop and a flutter they swing and sway,
And surge pell-mell down the Milky Way.
Betwixt the legs of the glittering Chair
They hover and squeak in the empty air.
Then round they swoop past the glimmering Lion
To where Sirius barks behind huge Orion;
Up, then, and over to wheel amain,
Under the silver, and home again.

Walter de la Mare

A-tishoo

'Sneeze, Pretty, sneeze, Dainty,
Else the Elves will have you sure;
Sneeze, Light-of-Seven-Bright-Candles,
See they're tippeting at the door;
Their wee feet in measure falling,
All their little voices calling,
Calling, calling, calling, calling—
Sneeze, or never come no more!'
        'A-tishoo!'

Walter de la Mare

A last word to Sharon before bed

As you tiptoe out of bed, slip
through the beckoning mirror
into your real nursery,
glide to the stars on the moon's prow;
remember to pay the toll
to the guardians—forty golden
winks they demand—or they'll slide the
black door shut behind you and
hold you hostage against
the breaking of the dawn.

Douglas Rome

Song

A lake and a fairy boat
To sail in the moonlight clear—
And merrily we would float
From the dragons that watch us here!

Thy gown should be snow-white silk,
And strings of orient pearls
Like gossamers dipped in milk
Should twine with thy raven curls!

Red rubies should deck thy hands,
And diamonds should be thy dower—
But Fairies have broken their wands
And wishing has lost its power!

Tom Hood

The old woman

There was an old woman tossed up in a basket,
Seventeen times as high as the moon;
And where she was going, I couldn't but ask it,
For in her hand she carried a broom.
Old woman, old woman, old woman, quoth I,
O whither, O whither, O whither so high?

To sweep the cobwebs off the sky!

Can I go with you?

      Aye, by and by.

Traditional

My tipi

The pictures on my tipi
Seem to come alive at night,
But when morning comes
They go to sleep again.

Laura Harlan

The old wife and the ghost

There was an old wife and she lived all alone
   In a cottage not far from Hitchin:
And one bright night, by the full moon light,
   Comes a ghost right into her kitchen.

About that kitchen neat and clean
   The ghost goes pottering round.
But the poor old wife is deaf as a boot
   And so hears never a sound.

The ghost blows up the kitchen fire,
   As bold as bold can be;
He helps himself from the larder shelf,
   But never a sound hears she.

He blows on his hands to make them warm,
   And whistles aloud 'Whee-hee!'
But still as a sack the old soul lies
   And never a sound hears she.

From corner to corner he runs about,
   And into the cupboard he peeps;
He rattles the door and bumps on the floor,
   But still the old wife sleeps.

Jangle and bang go the pots and pans,
   As he throws them all around;
And the plates and mugs and dishes and jugs,
   He flings them all to the ground.

Madly the ghost tears up and down
   And screams like a storm at sea;
And at last the old wife stirs in her bed—
   And it's 'Drat those mice,' says she.

Then the first cock crows and morning shows
    And the troublesome ghost's away.
But oh! what a pickle the poor wife sees
    When she gets up next day.

'Them's tidy big mice,' the old wife thinks,
    And off she goes to Hitchin,
And a tidy big cat she fetches back
    To keep the mice from her kitchen.

James Reeves

Topsyturvy world

If the butterfly courted the bee,
    And the owl the porcupine;
If churches were built in the sea,
    And three times one was nine;
If the pony rode the master,
    And the buttercups ate the cows,
If the cat had the dire disaster
    To be worried, sir, by the mouse;
If mamma, sir, sold the baby
    To a gipsy for half-a-crown;
If a gentleman, sir, was a lady,—
    The world would be Upside-Down!
If any or all of these wonders
    Should ever come about,
I should not consider them blunders,
    For I should be Inside-Out!

    Ba-ba, black wool,
        Have you any sheep?
    Yes, sir, a pack-ful,
        Creep, mouse, creep!

Four-and-twenty little maids
    Hanging out the pie,
Out jumped the honey-pot,
    Guy-Fawkes, Guy!
Cross-latch, cross-latch,
    Sit and spin the fire,
When the pie was opened,
    The bird was on the brier.

W. B. Rands

'Who are You?'
Says One to Two.
Says Two to One 'I'm plenty.'
'Think again!'
Says little Ten,
And, 'Think again!' says Twenty.

W. B. Rands

Friday night is my delight
And so is Saturday morning.
But Sunday night—it gives me a fright:
There's school on Monday morning.

Anon.

Oh, Joyce, Joyce, Joyce,
The cat's at the pies,
Poking with her forepaws
And gloating with her eyes!

Traditional

We're all in the dumps,
For diamonds are trumps,
The kittens are gone to St. Paul's,
The babies are bit,
The moon's in a fit,
And the houses are built without walls!

Traditional

All very odd

To see a bird pecking at fruit
　　Is nothing new.
But to see a dog playing a flute
　　Is very odd!

To see a Frenchman eating a frog
　　Is nothing new.
But to see a butcher chased by a hog
　　Is very odd!

To see a gardener gather a salad
　　Is nothing new.
But to see a donkey singing a ballad
　　Is very odd!

To see a man fish in a moat
　　Is nothing new.
But to see a monkey shaving a goat
　　Is very odd!

Traditional arranged by Geoffrey Summerfield

Index of authors

Index of first lines

Acknowledgements

For permission to reproduce copyright material the Editor is indebted to: George Allen and Unwin for **Oliphaunt** by J. R. R. Tolkien. Angus & Robertson (UK) Ltd for **Spanish Gold** from 'The Magic Pudding' by Norman Lindsay. Pat Ayers for **A Fishy Square Dance** from 'It Doesn't Always Have to Rhyme' and **What in the World** from 'There is no Rhyme for Silver' by Eve Merriam. James Britton for **If I had Forty Horsemen** and **June** by James Britton. William Rossa Cole for **Oh, Who Will Wash the Tiger's Ears** by Shel Silverstein copyright © 1967 by the author. Cresset Press for **Cider In the Potting Shed** and **The Celebrated Cat: Purser O'Hara** by Ruth Pitter. Faber and Faber Ltd for **The Yak** from 'Collected Poems of Theodore Roethke'. Robert Graves for **Henry and Mary** and **Allie** from 'Collected Poems' by Robert Graves. Thom Gunn for **See saw**. Harper & Row Publishers Inc. for **At the Playground** from 'Stories that Could be True: New and Collected Poems by William Stafford' copyright © 1977 by the author and **Magic, The Acrobats, Boa Constrictor, Ickle Me, Pickle Me, Tickle Me Too, Invisible Boy** and **It's Dark in Here** from 'Where the Sidewalk Ends' by Shel Silverstein copyright © 1974 by the author. William Heinemann Ltd for **Grim and Gloomy** by James Reeves. Michael Joseph for **Cottage** from 'Then There Were Three' by Eleanor Farjeon. The Estate of Dilys Laing and Harold Matson Co. Inc. for **Little Bright One** and **Blackout** by Dilys Laing. Little, Brown and Company for **Eletelephony** from 'Tirra Lirra' by Laura E. Richards. George MacBeth for **Noah's Journey** by George MacBeth. The Executors of the Mac-Diarmid Estate for **Hungry Waters** and **The Bubblyjock and Turkeycock** by Hugh MacDiarmid. Macmillan Ltd for **I saw a Jolly Hunter** and **Tom Bone** from 'Figgie Hobbin' by Charles Causley. The Literary Trustees of Walter de la Mare and The Society of Authors for **A-Tishoo, John Mouldy, Who Really? The Hare, Alas, Alack, Hi!** and **Crumbs** by Walter de la Mare. Methuen Children's Books for **Bad Sir Brian Botany** from 'When We Were Very Young' and **Solitude** from 'Now We Are Six' by A. A. Milne, Pete Morgan for **So Wide** by Pete Morgan. New